NATIONAL
GEOGRAPHIC

Mud, Mud, Mud

Dot Meharry

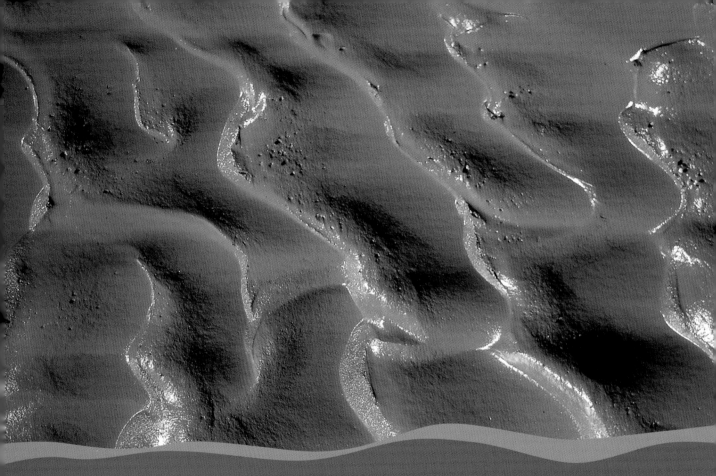

Mud is soft.

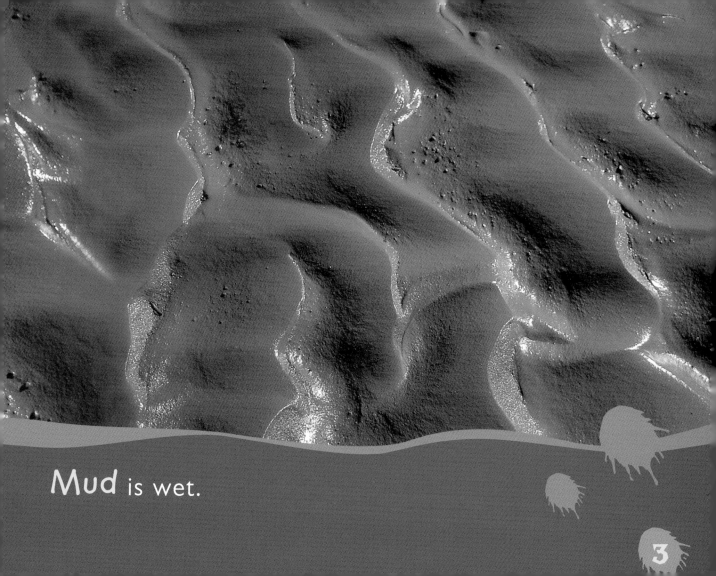

Mud is wet.

A pig likes mud.

A pig rolls in the **mud**.
The **mud** helps keep the pig cool.

A frog likes **mud**.

A frog sleeps in the **mud**.
The **mud** helps a frog hide from its enemies.

A water buffalo likes mud.

A water buffalo stands in the mud.
The mud helps keep bugs away.

A rhinoceros likes **mud**.

A rhinoceros has a **mud** bath.

The **mud** helps protect the rhinoceros from the sun.

What else likes **mud**?